BERKLEE PRESS

CD Included

Beyond Bluegrass Banjo

Etudes and Ideas for the Modern Banjo Player

by Dave Hollender and Matt Glaser

Edited by Jonathan Feist

Berklee Press

Vice President: David Kusek
Dean of Continuing Education: Debbie Cavalier
Chief Operating Officer: Robert F. Green
Managing Editor: Jonathan Feist
Editorial Assistants: Martin Fowler, Amy Kaminski, Andrea Penzel, Jacqueline Sim
Assistant to Matt Glaser: Susan Buzzard
Cover Designer: Eric Gould

All music is copyright Matt's Music, 2009, with the exception of "The Girl I Left Behind Me."

ISBN 978-0-87639-118-1

1140 Boylston Street
Boston, MA 02215-3693 USA
(617) 747-2146

Visit Berklee Press Online at
www.berkleepress.com

DISTRIBUTED BY

HAL•LEONARD®
CORPORATION
7777 W. BLUEMOUND RD. P.O. BOX 13819
MILWAUKEE, WISCONSIN 53213

Visit Hal Leonard Online at
www.halleonard.com

CONTENTS

CD TRACKS

Musicians

Dave Hollender, Banjo

John McGann, Mandolin and Guitar

Jim Whitney, Bass

Matt Glaser, Violin (Tracks 1 and 2)

Jimmy Ryan, Mandolin (Tracks 1 and 2)

Tony Trischka, Banjo (Tracks 1 and 2)

Recorded at Arbor Vitae Studios (John McGann, Engineer) and Blue Heron Studio

DAVE'S PREFACE

Matt and I each heard many kinds of music at home and, in spite of the fact that bluegrass was not part of our parents' record collections, we each began playing it in our teens. Our interests led us to branch out into jazz and other styles and I took up bass as a second instrument, mainly for two reasons. I wanted to study at Berklee and they didn't offer banjo, and I realized that every kind of music includes a bass, so it would lead to more opportunities. That proved right. Paradoxically, it both deepened my enjoyment and appreciation of straight-ahead banjo playing, while at the same time, playing other kinds of music offered lessons that contributed many ideas to my approach to banjo. Which brings us to this book.

You will find *Beyond Bluegrass Banjo* to be quite different from most "banjo books." Most teach fundamental techniques, or they are collections of tunes, transcriptions, or licks. This book is a collection of tunes, each of which is designed to demonstrate a particular musical concept or technique. They are, in a sense, generic, in that they are concepts that can be applied to bluegrass or any other style of music. The intent is to offer material that you will use for working out arrangements, improvising, and composing tunes.

With few exceptions the banjo parts are close to the exact lines that Matt composed. They will definitely challenge your instrumental skills and are examples of ways that music originally played on another instrument can be played on banjo. On the repeats of tunes, I took more liberties in order to demonstrate other options and create variations on tunes.

MATT'S PREFACE

Welcome to a book of etudes, exercises, and ideas that will help you develop your technical and musical skills in the world of contemporary banjo. The world of acoustic string music has exploded in the last twenty years, thanks largely to the efforts of players like Mark O'Conner, Béla Fleck, and Chris Thile, who have demonstrated that it's possible to play various forms of bluegrass, jazz, and contemporary classical music, all at a very high technical level, and sometimes even simultaneously! I have been part of this world for a long time, teaching at both Mark's and Jay Ungar's camps since their inception. For twenty-eight years, I have observed (and participated in) the scene from my post as chair of the string department at Berklee College of Music.

Over the last few years, I have tried to focus my teaching to help my students develop compositional and intellectual skills applied to their instrument, in real time. Put another way, musicians should not be automatons, letting their fingers run rampant. Instead, they should have a comprehensive mental map of music in their heads, as well as a wide range of musical skills that would make them employable in a band setting. The exercises and etudes in this book are designed to help you grow technically on your instrument, while at the same time develop a comprehensive understanding of the inner workings of music.

Some of the etudes in this book are designed to help you grow melodically, others harmonically, and others rhythmically. Melody, harmony, and rhythm are the three elements of music, and as a contemporary improviser, you will need to find methods that help you grow in each of these areas.

SOME WORDS ABOUT THESE ARRANGEMENTS

To preserve the content of the lessons in this book I have tried to include as many details as possible when arranging the fiddle melodies for banjo. However, the fingerings and techniques I played are just one of any number of possible solutions that could have been used to play this music. So, they should be seen as just that: one player's solution. After you have explored my arrangements, I urge you to experiment, modify, embellish, and substitute your own ideas.

NOTATION AND NOMENCLATURE

All arrangements in this book use 3-finger technique with the banjo tuned to either gDGBd or aDGBd. The tuning and any use of a capo are indicated for each piece. The standard music notation is all written one octave higher than the actual sounding pitches.[1]

The terminology in this book presumes some knowledge of theory, particularly chord construction. If you've never studied music theory or don't know how to interpret standard notation, we suggest getting started with a book such as *Berklee Music Theory*, by Paul Schmeling. It will really help you to better understand and apply these lessons.

ABBREVIATIONS

Letters below tablature indicate picking fingers and certain articulations

> I – index
> M – middle
> T – thumb
> S – slide
> H – hammer
> P – pull-off
> Ch – choke or string bend

Numbers above tablature indicate fretting fingers

> 0 – open
> 1 – index
> 2 – middle
> 3 – ring
> 4 – pinky
> T – thumb

---

1   This transposition is done to reduce the number of ledger lines that must be used. It is standard practice on guitar and is how classic style banjo music published during the late nineteenth and early twentieth century was written.

PLAYING ALONG WITH THE CD

The CD accompanying this book includes performances of all the etudes featuring the banjo with full band and those same tracks without the banjo. *How* you practice can have more affect on your progress than how *much* you practice. I want you to keep two things in mind.

1. ***Slower is faster.***

Before even putting on your picks, you should listen to the tracks a number of times while visually following along with the music. Then play it slowly, section by section, to learn the notes. When you have the notes under your fingers start to play with the track. I recommend slowing the tracks down and looping sections, then gradually speeding them up.[2]

Each time you play, you create or reinforce muscle memories that will either work for you or work against you. If you make a mistake in the same spot two or three times, that is important information. It is easy to "groove" or reinforce that kind of mistake. The solution is to isolate it and play it until you get it right ten times in a row. I guarantee that this will take less time than trying to fix it later.

2. ***You can't practice something until after you have learned it.***

Once you know the part well, play along with the track many times. At that point, you should focus your attention on *details* and *how* you are playing. This is all about *awareness*. Notice things like the time feel, the relationship of the banjo to the other parts, etc. This is only possible after you know the notes well enough that your mental energy is not consumed by trying to remember the tune.

TRACK 1   TRACK 2

The first two tracks on the CD feature two of the songs we study later, presented as they would be in an extended performance. The other tracks are designed to focus more on the banjo part so that you can isolate the techniques I present.

The recorded performances of most of these tunes include variations in repeated sections of tunes. Many of these variations are written out, but some small changes on repeats are not on the page. This really is the primary message of the book: that you should be able to find the core of a melody and make up variations on that core melody, while retaining its shape. Study the variations to get ideas for doing this on your own. Let's get started.

---

2   There are computer applications that can change the speed of audio files without changing the pitch and let you create loops. Two I have experience with are Transcribe! (www.seventhstring.com) and Amazing Slow Downer (www.ronimusic.com).

CHAPTER 1

Lamb Chops (Skeletal Melody and the Five Levels of Improvisation)

Learning to improvise on a melody is a core message of this book. There are many methods that teach you to improvise on the chords, or underlying harmony of a tune, and that is certainly an important approach. But central to any kind of folk or country improvisation is the ability to identify the essential elements in a melody and improvise on them.

THE FIVE LEVELS OF IMPROVISATION

"The Five Levels of Improvisation" is an idea inspired by the great alto saxophonist Lee Konitz, who teaches a gradual development of a melody that he calls "The Ten Levels of Improvisation." We have taken this approach, modified and developed it, and organized it so that it may be of value to folks playing music other than jazz.

Before you do anything else, you should try to identify the song's *skeletal melody*. As our musical example, we're going to start with the familiar children's tune "Mary Had a Little Lamb" (don't laugh). You may not think very highly of this melody, but you'd be wrong! Tunes like this have gotten rid of every extraneous element, and have been subjected to what scientists call "Occam's Razor." This principle stipulates that one should not needlessly multiply explanations when fewer would suffice. Simpler is usually better. Tunes such as "Mary Had a Little Lamb" are nicely boiled down to a very simple but valuable progression of pitches. Even so, your first step in improvising on this simple melody is to boil it down even further and try to find a simple skeleton of pitches.

The following examples are presented on track 3 of the CD. Track 4 mutes the banjo part so that you can practice playing along.

 "Lamb Chops" Full Band
TRACK 3

 "Lamb Chops" Play Along
TRACK 4

Level 1. Connect with Quarter Notes

Level 1 of our five levels of improvisation is to connect these skeletal tones with constantly moving quarter notes.

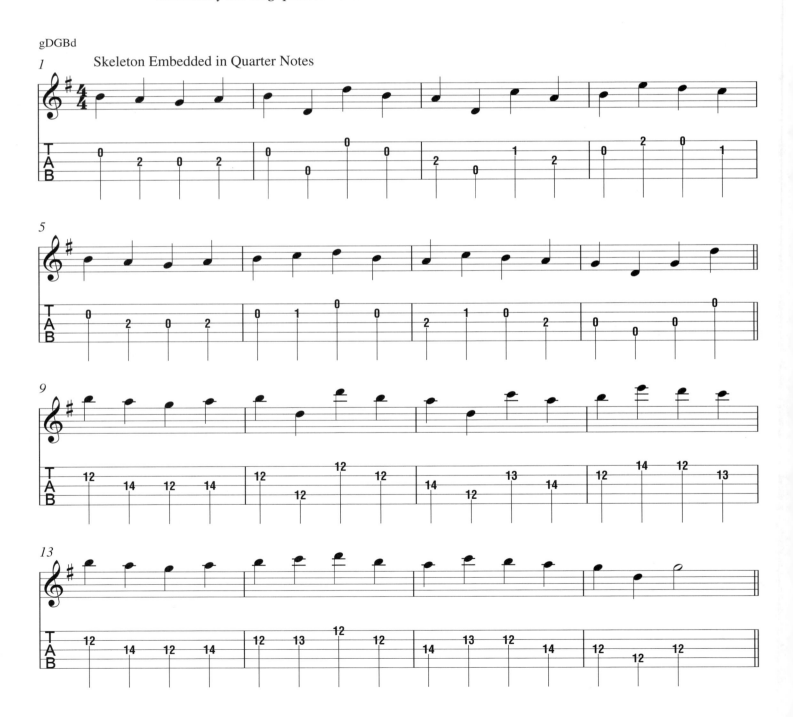

Igor Stravinsky wrote in *Poetics of Music*:

My freedom thus consists in my moving about within the narrow frame that I have assigned myself for each one of my undertakings. I shall go even further: my freedom will be so much the greater and more meaningful the more narrowly I limit my field of action and the more I surround myself with obstacles. Whatever diminishes constraint, diminishes strength. The more constraints one imposes, the more one frees one's self of the chains that shackle the spirit.

In this case of the skeletal melody concept, restricting and limiting the field of action paradoxically gives us the freedom to make one small creative gesture.

In "Lamb Chops," we'd like you to play constantly moving quarter notes on the skeletal melody, but only in steps; that is, restrict the way you connect the pitches to stepwise motion—no leaps. That will be level 1A. Level 1B will be for you to connect the skeletal melody in constantly moving quarter notes in leaps—no steps. Finally, level 1C will be for you to connect the skeletal melody in constantly moving quarter notes with some chromaticism added.

Level 2. Constantly Moving Eighth Notes

Keeping the same skeletal melody, you're now going to apply constantly moving eighth notes. Level 2 A, B, and C are as above. In each case, connect the skeletal melody with constantly moving eighth notes (a) in steps, (b) in leaps, and (c) with chromaticism. Here is an eighth note line written out in two different octaves.

Matt Glaser
Arr. Dave Hollender

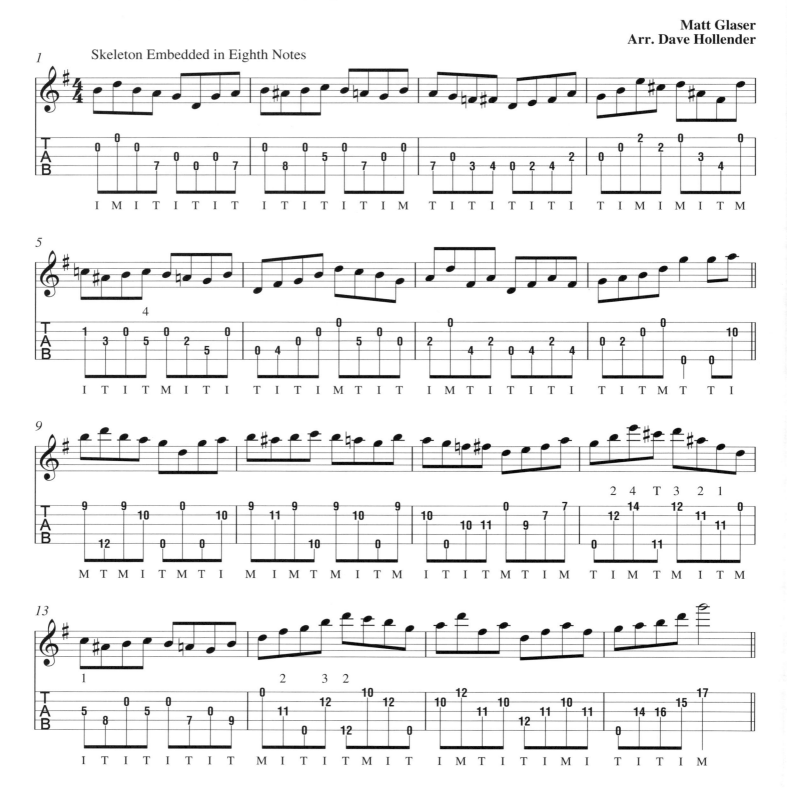

Skeleton Embedded in Eighth Notes

Level 3. Rhythmic Variations

In level 3, we'll ask you to shift your focus slightly, and make up rhythmic variations on the skeletal melody.

In the first two levels, you were restricted rhythmically to playing constantly moving quarters or eighths. Here you're free to play any rhythms you want as long as you play the skeletal melody.

Matt Glaser

Level 4. Counterpoint

Level 4 asks you to play counterpoint to a melody. This is an extremely important but rarely discussed component of great improvisers in any idiom. The best way to begin thinking about this level is to imagine a band with a singer, where some instrumentalist is playing tasty backup while the singer sings.

That tasty backup is essentially counterpoint to a melody. Your counterpoint should be relatively still while the melody is moving, and relatively active while the melody is still. You should get to the point where you can keep a melody going in your head while playing counterpoint on your instrument. This bifurcated hearing is something that exists in all styles of music other than western classical. To practice this, I recommend you record yourself playing a melody, and then play that recording back at a medium volume while improvising a counterpoint. Over time, you should gradually turn the volume down on your recording until you can keep it going entirely in your head without reference to an external audio source.

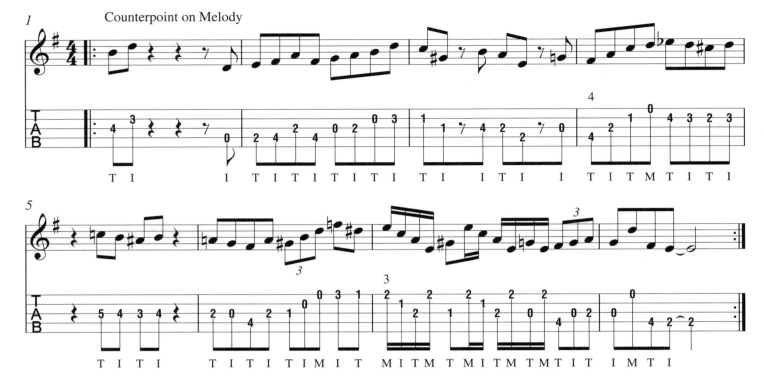

Level 5. Abstraction

Finally, we come to level 5. This level asks you to make a conceptual leap and imagine the eight bars of "Mary…" as a frame in which you are to improvise. Matt will often ask a student to make a short abstract drawing and then try to play that visual abstraction in the frame of the eight bars of this tune.

These five principles are applicable to any style of music. All you need to do is to find the skeletal melody of whatever you're improvising on, and then follow these simple rules. We have worked with people using these ideas on fiddle tunes like "Arkansas Traveler," on jazz standards like "All the Things You Are," and even on movements from the Bach unaccompanied violin sonatas.

The performance track on the CD begins with constantly moving quarter notes, and goes through jazz phrasing of a melody. You may practice the remaining levels with the play-along track.

CHAPTER 2

The Girl I Left Behind Me (Reharmonization)

"The Girl I Left Behind Me" is a very beautiful old tune, just as evocative now as when it was first composed. Like most fiddle tunes, the overall form is AABB, in which every letter represents eight bars of music. Its well-known melody has even been quoted in solos by jazz pianist Thelonious Monk and the great Louis Armstrong, who quotes it in a vocal number entitled, "Rhythm Saved the World."

The focus of our version of this great old Civil War–era tune is to hear a familiar melody played against the backdrop of more active and unexpected chord changes—what jazz players call a *reharmonization*. Making up your own "re-harms" is a good way to exercise your ear, although you may incur the wrath of more traditional friends!

It starts with typical alternating bass notes and chords with typical triads, not too different from what Earl might have played, followed at letter B with chords that include the 6th or 7th. The 6th chords and passing diminished chords suggest a Texas-style accompaniment. The rolls in the second chorus have a more bluegrass feel. At letter F, I included another example of improvised *counterpoint* around the fiddle melody.

Be sure to notice the effect of the D pedal in the B section. It creates an open feeling that provides an effective foil to the harmonic rhythm in the A sections. The contrast and transitions help generate feelings of ***tension and release*** in the music, something that is key to playing great solos. This is just one way to achieve it, and you should begin to notice it when you are listening and playing.

TRACK 5 "The Girl I Left Behind Me" Full Band

 TRACK 6 "The Girl I Left Behind Me" Play Along

The Girl I Left Behind Me

Arr. Dave Hollender
Matt Glaser

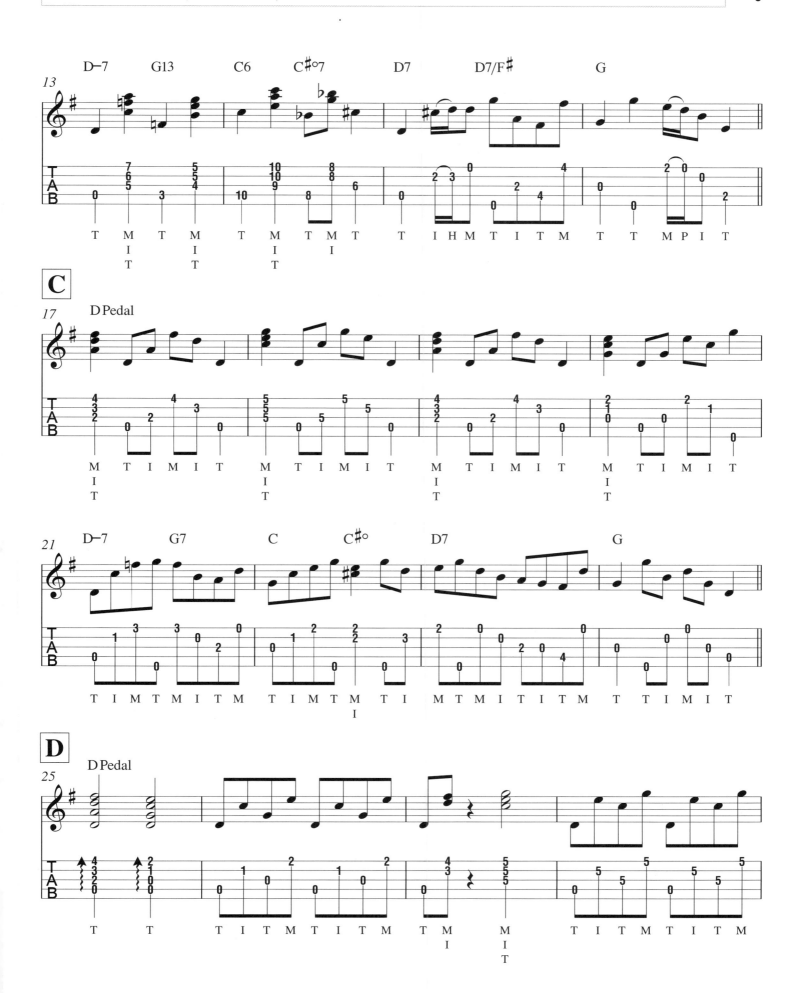

The Infinite Blackberry Blossom (Melodic Cells and Progressive Rhythmic Variation)

Next, we will explore progressive rhythmic variation. "The Infinite Blackberry Blossom," or as Dave calls it, "Pachelbel's Blackberry Blossom," applies these principles to a descending major scale.

Melodies based on descending major scales are ubiquitous. The fiddle tune "Blackberry Blossom" could be reduced to a descending major scale as its core melody.

> *I was never very good at math in school, but the other day I was trying to figure out a math problem related to this tune. If you had twenty distinct variations of a melodic idea, each one four eighth-notes long, how many different ways could you combine these variations on "Blackberry Blossom?" Since there are seven notes in the descending scale, and twenty of these little melodies, I believe the answer would be 7 to the 20th power, which is an incredibly large number that's fifteen digits long. Don't worry, I'm not asking you to play all these variations, nor would it even be possible. My point is simply that starting with very simple materials in combination, you can quickly generate a vast amount of material for creativity.*
> —M.G.

There's an old story that illustrates this concept. The court jester and the king were playing chess, and the court jester won. The king said, "I must pay you handsomely for your win." The jester said, "I don't need much. Just put a penny on the first square of the chessboard, then two pennies on the next, then keep doubling the number of pennies on each square as you go." The king said, "Oh, that can't be enough. I need to pay you more." And the jester said, "Don't worry, that'll be fine."

The answer, needless to say, is an extremely high number. The total amount of money on the chessboard is—hold onto your hats—$184,467,440,737,095,516.15.

That jester was crazy like a fox.

If you look at the music for "The Infinite Blackberry Blossom," you will see that in bar 17, we begin using eighth notes, and every four bars, I introduce a new, very simple melodic idea. I call these melodic ideas "cells." You should practice constructing your own melodic cells and playing them on every step of a descending major scale. At the very end of the music, and at the end of the CD track, you'll hear me begin to play triplets. Try to explore playing triplets on your own, using the same idea of melodic cells. Next, try playing melodic cells in sixteenth notes.

🔊 **"The Infinite Blackberry Blossom" Full Band**
TRACK 7

🔊 **"The Infinite Blackberry Blossom" Play Along**
TRACK 8

The Infinite Blackberry Blossom

Matt Glaser
Arr. by Dave Hollender

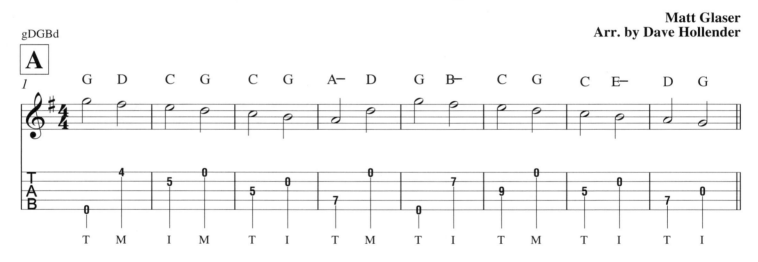

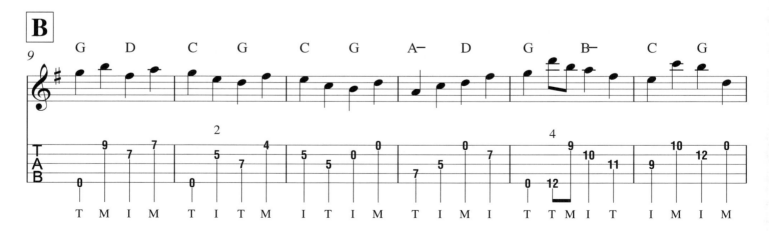

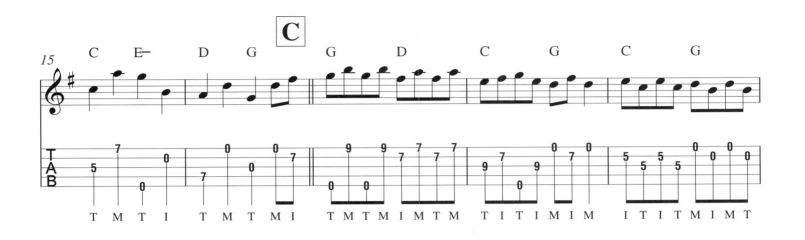

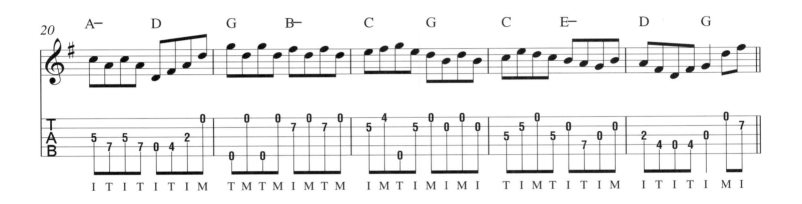

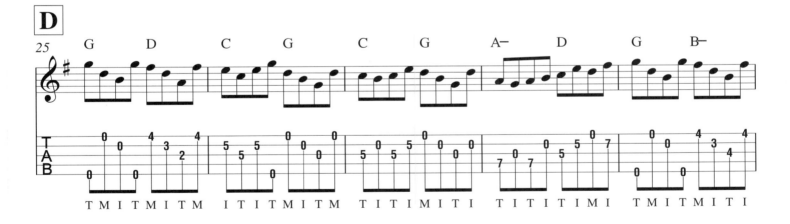

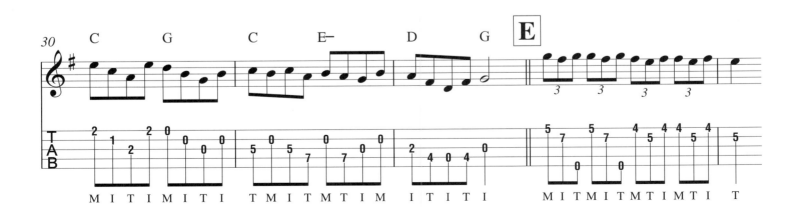

CHAPTER 4

The Ark and the Saw (Changing the Mode)

The first fiddle tune I learned when I took up the instrument at the age of thirteen was "Arkansas Traveler." I've been playing the fiddle for forty years, and I'm still obsessed with this tune.
—M.G.

This brings to mind a beautiful poem by Walt Whitman:

Beginning my studies the first step pleas'd me so much,
The mere fact consciousness, these forms, the power of motion,
The least insect or animal, the senses, eyesight, love,
The first step I say awed me and pleas'd me so much,
I have hardly gone and hardly wish'd to go any farther,
But stop and loiter all the time to sing it in ecstatic songs.

In any case, it's a great tune!

This variation on "Arkansas Traveler," called "The Ark and the Saw," throws a number of different compositional techniques into the mix. When you understand these principles, try to apply them to a tune of your choice.

The first thing is to maintain the general shape of the melody, as we have discussed in other chapters.

Next, the mode has been changed—in other words, the scale that was used. Normally, "Arkansas Traveler" uses the notes in a major scale. This variation is based on a pentatonic scale: D, E, G, A, and C, which is a mode of a C major pentatonic scale. It does use other notes in the variation, but those five notes are at the core of what's going on here.

In addition to changing the mode, the melody is fanned out over two octaves. Whenever you're working on a tune, you should always begin by playing the melody in its original location—its original octave. Then, try to play the entire melody either down or up an octave, as the case may be. Finally, you should make up a variation that combines both octaves. This will necessitate making up new melodic material to link the two octaves together.

You'll notice that the second variation is highly abstract, bearing only the slimmest relationship to the original core melody. It is frequently fleshed out with references to open strings. If you experiment with putting in open strings randomly in the middle of melodies, you'll create unexpected interval patterns. Also notice that the timbre (tone color) of open-string notes can be quite different than those of fingered notes. As long as you're aware of it, it can be a positive attribute to use as an effect.

Although the recorded performance on the CD contains the same B section both times through the tune, we've given you an extra B section variation in the music notation. This variation is similar to what was played on the extended performance, which is CD track 1.

"The Ark and the Saw" Full Band

TRACK 9

"The Ark and the Saw" Play Along

TRACK 10

The Ark and the Saw

Matt Glaser
Arr. Dave Hollender

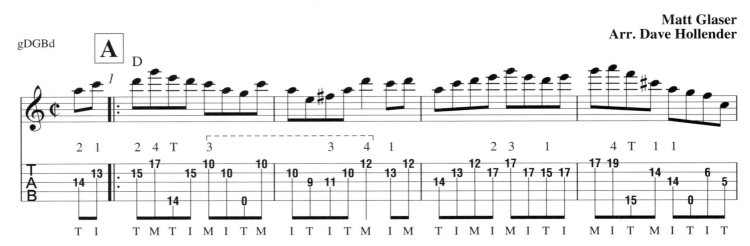

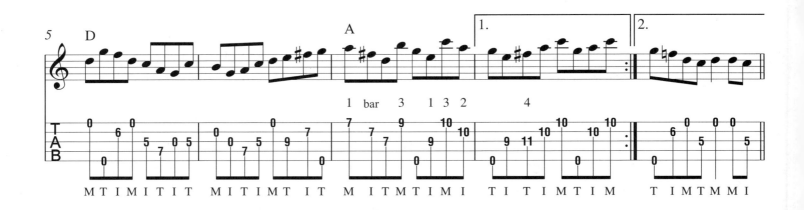

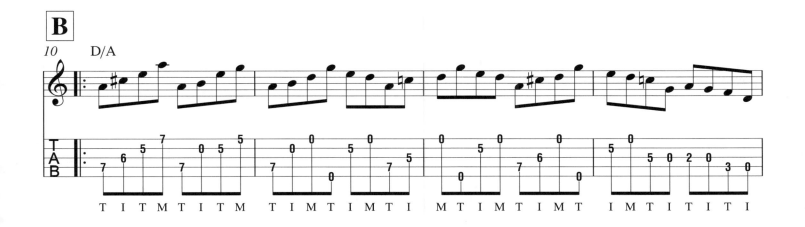

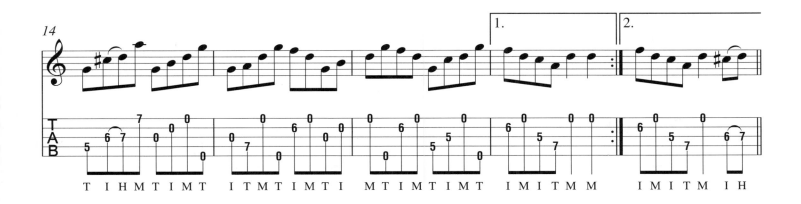

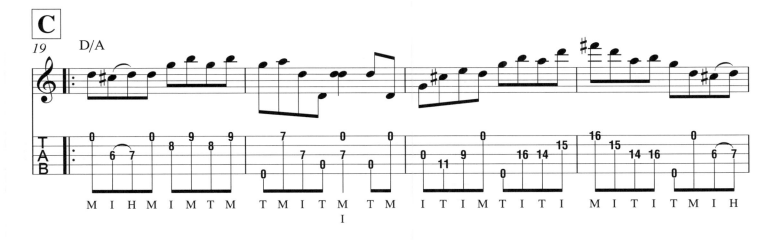

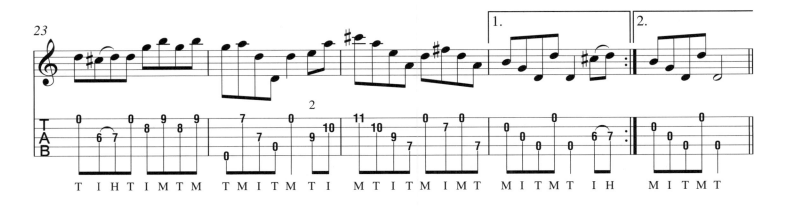

D

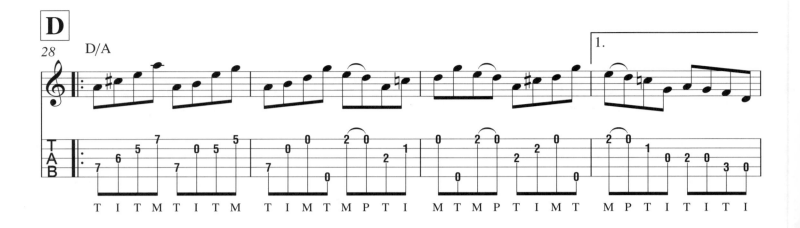

E

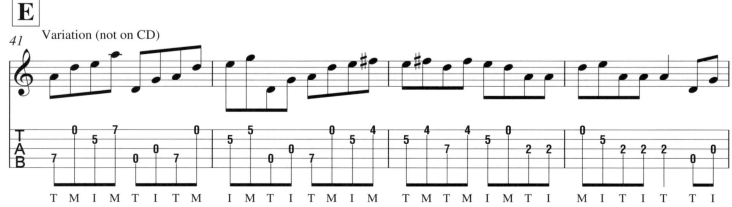

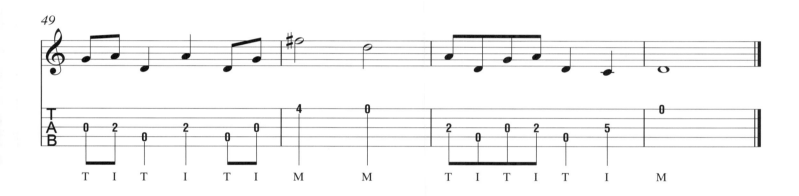

CHAPTER 5

Act Natural (Mutually Exclusive Triads)

There's a great scene in a documentary about the bluegrass singer Jimmy Martin in which Jimmy is plagued by a heckler in the audience. Jimmy says to this fellow, "If you want to horse around with me, we can go out back. I'll be the horse's head, and you just act natural."

> *When I heard that line, I knew I had to write a tune called "Act Natural." Anyone who has ever heard me play knows that I have a predilection for quoting the Bill Monroe tune "Wheel Hoss." To combine the horse imagery in the anecdote with the tune "Wheel Hoss" seemed an opportunity too good to pass up. So here is "Act Natural."*
> *—M.G.*

The tune "Wheel Hoss" itself is very Mixolydian in character, with its strong emphasis on the flatted 7th degree of the scale. We've taken that basic concept and developed it here. You'll notice that the first part of this tune is based on what are called "mutually exclusive triads." Don't be scared; this just means two alternating chords, one of which shares *none* of the notes in the other chord. This melody begins by alternating notes in the G major triad with notes in the F major triad, which don't have any notes in common. It then follows these chords in their inversions going up the scale.

The bridge of this tune offers much needed contrast from the unrelenting eighth notes of the A section by having a more lyrical, sustained bluegrass melody.

 "Act Natural" Full Band

TRACK 11

 "Act Natural" Play Along

TRACK 12

Act Natural

Matt Glaser
Arr. Dave Hollender

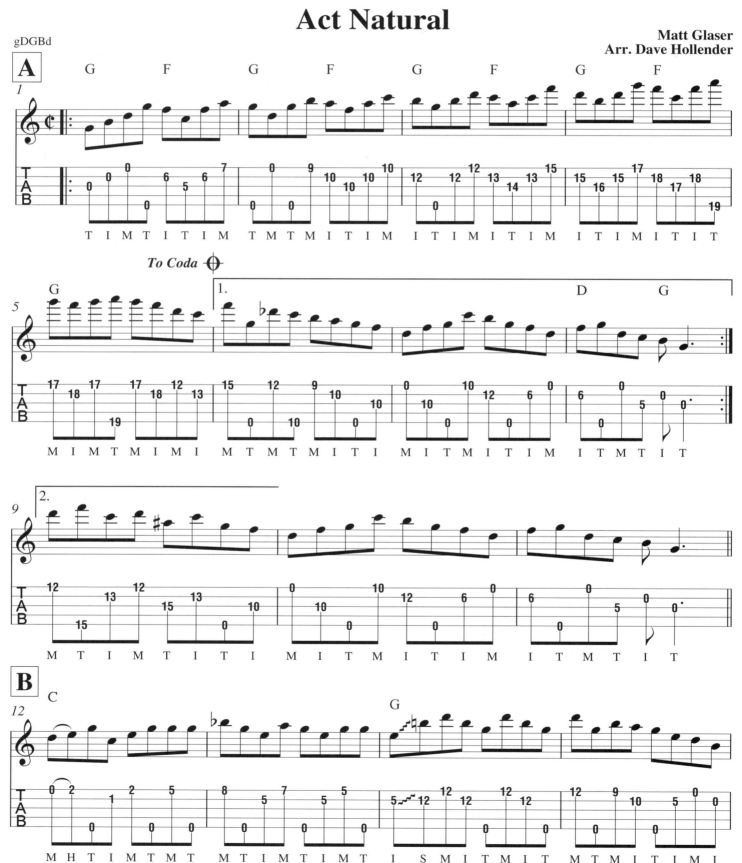

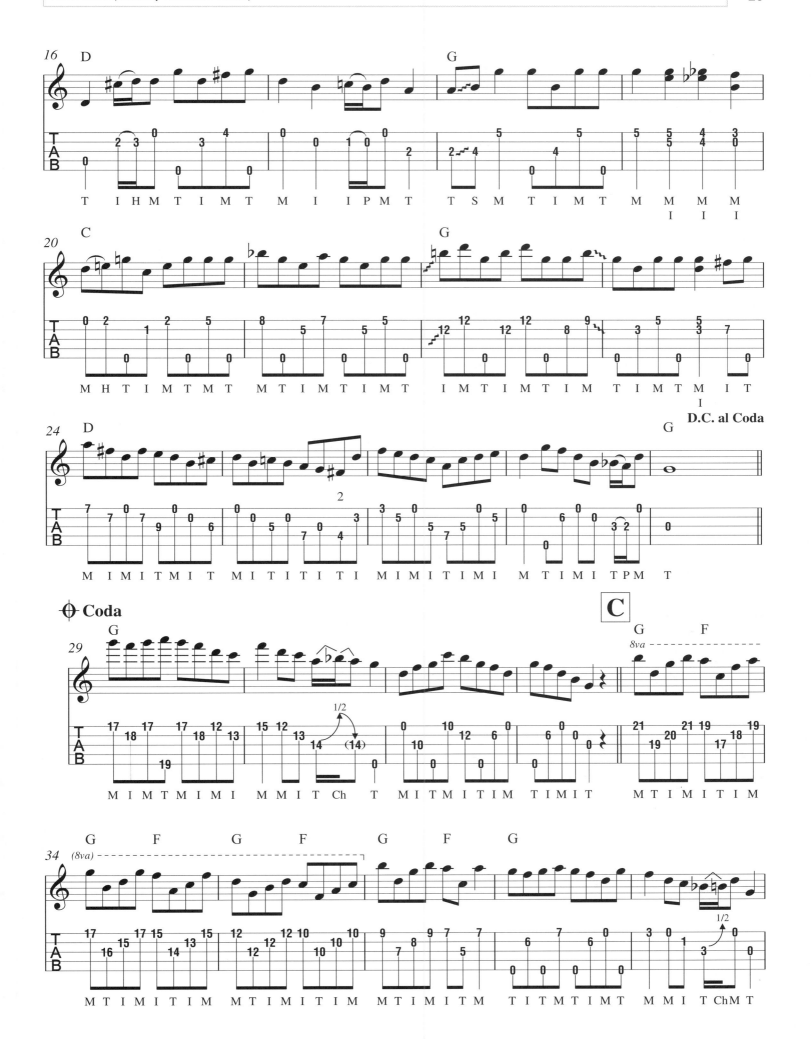

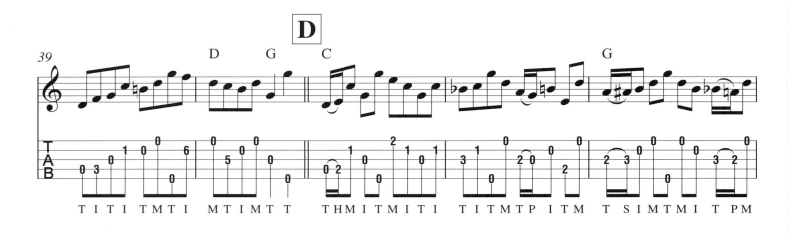

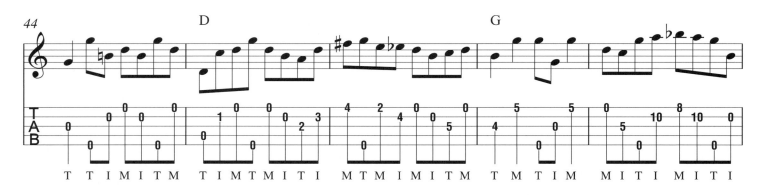

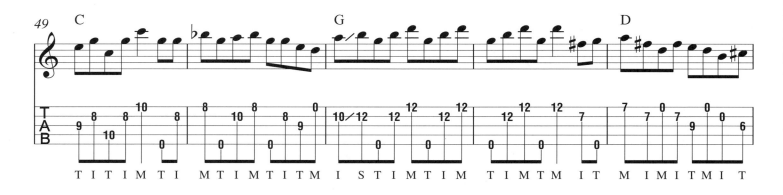

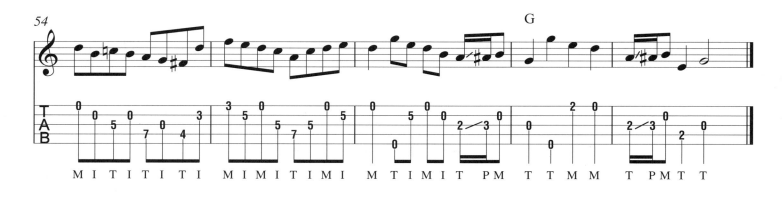

High Windy (Developing Motifs and Upper-Structure Triads)

I wrote "High Windy" in 1990 for a friend of mine, Julia Weatherford. Julia and her family live in the mountains near Ashville, N.C. They specifically live on a mountain called "High Windy." I thought this was too good a bluegrass fiddle tune name to pass up. "High Windy," like many other tunes, has a core Mixolydian identity, but is also inundated with chromatic-approach tones and upper-structure triads—3-note chords that include one or more chord tensions (beyond the 7th).
—M.G.

You'll see that the structure of the A section of "High Windy" is based on a repeating melodic motif, which exists in bars 1, 5, 9, and 13. Each time, the answer to that initial statement climbs higher and higher.

- The first answer is in bar 2 and goes as high as a C natural.
- The next answer is in bar 6 and goes up to D natural.
- The next answer is in bar 10 and goes up to E natural.
- Finally, the climactic phrase of the A section is in bar 14, which goes up to B natural before coming to rest on a G sharp.

The last three notes of bar 14 are E, B, and G♯, which spell an E major triad. In the key of D, an E major triad is considered an upper-structure triad, built using the 9, ♯11, and 13. An upper-structure triad can be major or minor. In this case, it's a major triad, created by using ♯11.

Another way to look at the same melodic material would be as scale degrees. Looking at bar 14 this way, the notes would be 1, 3, 5, ♭7, 9, 13, and ♯11.

Always be conscious of what scale degree you are playing. Also, be aware of what key you're in at the moment, and what scale degree you are playing relative to that key. This awareness will help focus your playing and add clarity to your improvisations.

In other words, *play in the key, not in the chord*. What this means is that it's less important that you know every single chord change in a tune, but more important that you know the key of the moment.

The melody of the B section creates variety in a different manner from that of the A section. Here, we have a 2-bar motif that develops on gradually ascending degrees of the scale. The melody of the first two bars is oriented around D. Starting at bar 19, the two bars are oriented around E, and starting at bar 21, those two bars are oriented around F♯. The descending lick, which begins in bar 23, is an adaptation of a famous phrase by the great tenor saxophonist Lester Young, from his solo on the tune "Jive at Five" with the Count Basie Orchestra.

It's worth noting the effect of the chords in the B section too. It starts on a D, which is followed by E/D, a hybrid chord. That pedal tone exerts a powerful effect on the music, giving it a static quality with a feeling of suspense that is then resolved in the bars that follow. It also works great on banjo since you can use open 4th string in a roll to provide that note.

Some of the elements in the transcription can be found in the extended performance of "High Windy," which is CD track 2.

 "High Windy" Full Band

TRACK 13

 "High Windy" Play Along

TRACK 14

High Windy

Matt Glaser
Arr. Dave Hollender

gDGBd

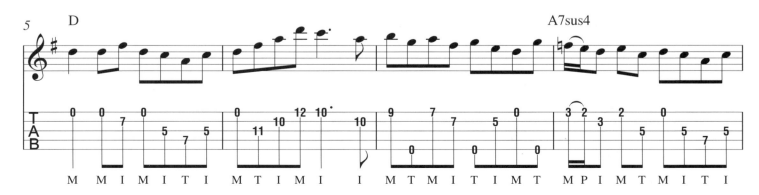

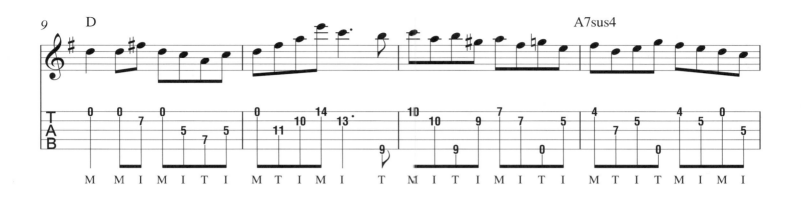

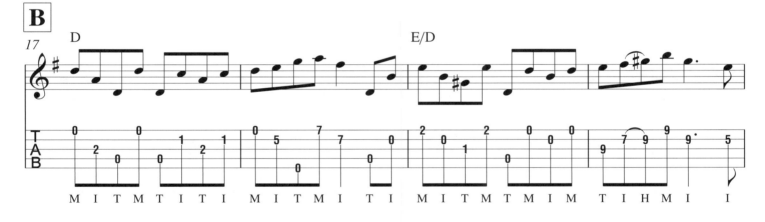

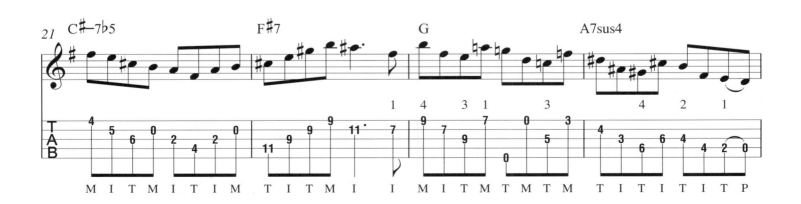

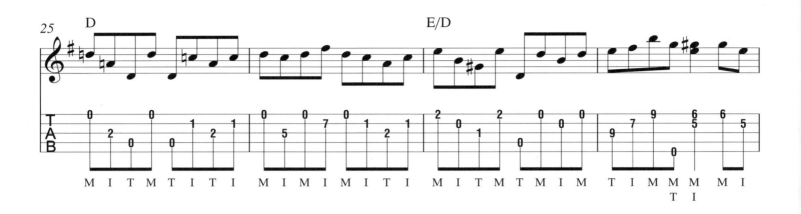

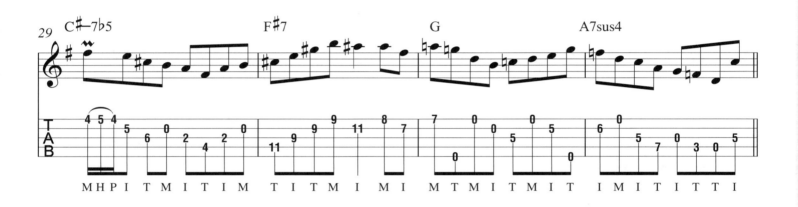

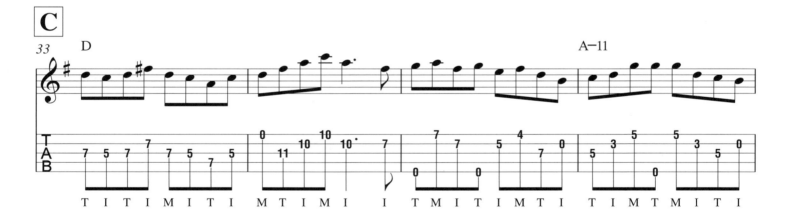

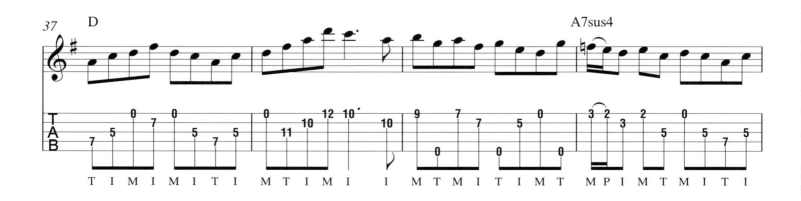

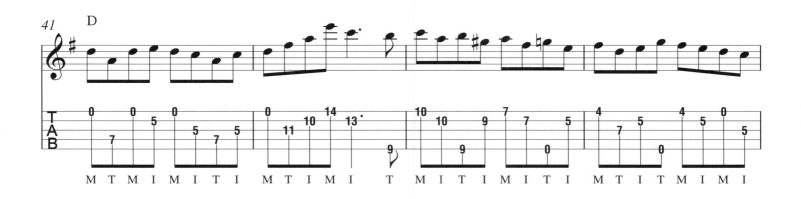

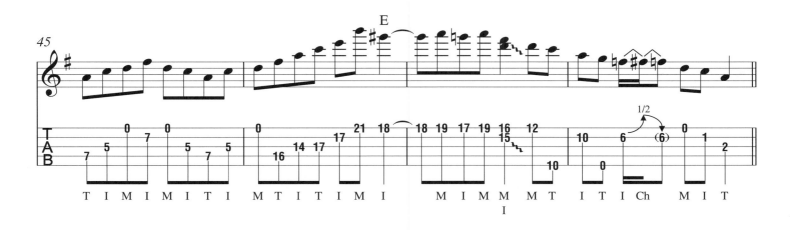

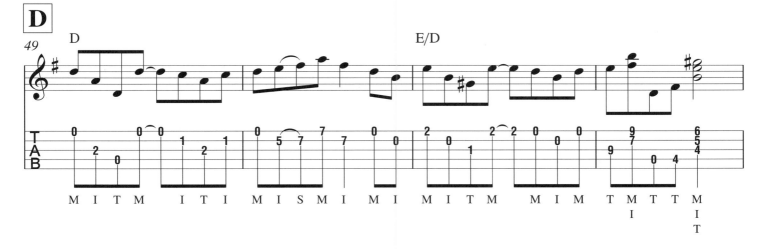

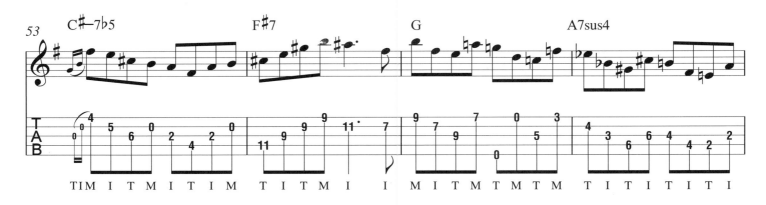

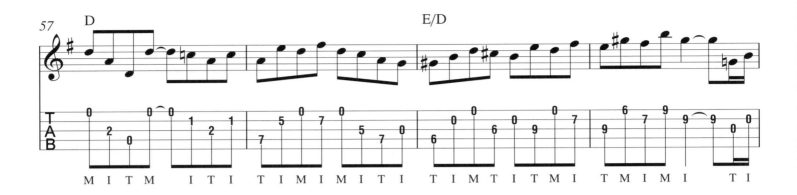

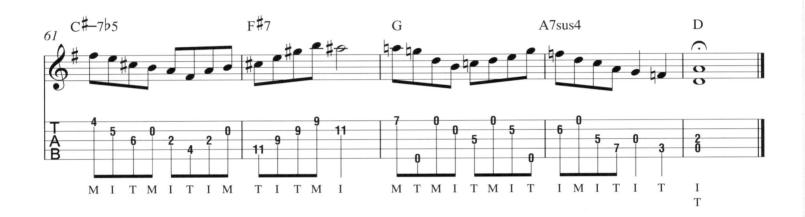

CHAPTER 7

IHOP (Mixolydian Melody)

The title of this tune is an acronym, but it does not stand for International House of Pancakes. It also does not stand for "I have omnipotent power," "I have orange pants," "I'm happy optimistic person," or "I hate over-playing." If you think you know what this acronym stands for, please e-mail Matt your suggestions at mglaser@berklee.edu. If you are the winner, you will receive an e-mail from Matt Glaser!

This tune is in the key of B, but the melody is based on a Mixolydian sound: a major scale but with a flat 7th scale degree. In this regard, the tune is similar to "Hot Lick Fiddle Chick," "Act Natural," and many traditional tunes that all share a Mixolydian modality.

The melody to "IHOP" is almost a Rubik's Cube of interlocking melodic elements. The opening two bars form the core melody, which is then transplanted to the B chord, and then to the F♯ chord.

The bridge of this tune has more of a classical, victorious, Bill Monroe vibe. Notice how a change in the melodic rhythm dramatically alters the feeling of the tune. Instead of constantly running eighth notes as in the A section, the bridge has varied rhythms which are more vocal in character, and the high pitch contributes to its exultant quality. Be careful of the double chromatic-approach tones, a landmine that this tune shares with "Hot Lick Fiddle Chick."

In measures 38 to 40, I inserted a little taste of a technique called "side-slipping." A fragment of the melody is played and then transposed up a half step, then back down. This is a favorite technique of horn players but not often heard on banjo. The transposed version sounds a little "warped," but it works because of two things: it is a repetition of the previous statement, and it is promptly resolved back to the original pitches.

I'm told John Hartford said, "Music is based on repetition." A truer statement about music has never been spoken!

"IHOP" Full Band

TRACK 15

"IHOP" Play Along

TRACK 16

IHOP

Matt Glaser
Arr. Dave Hollender

gDGBd
Capo 4

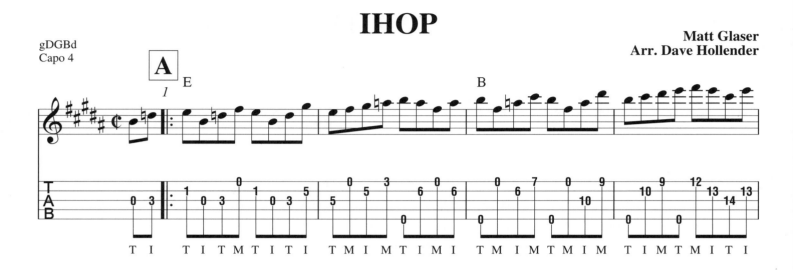

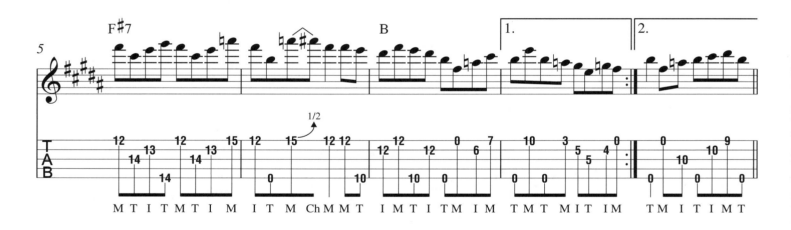

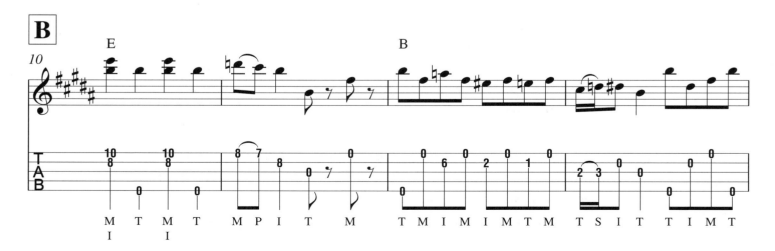

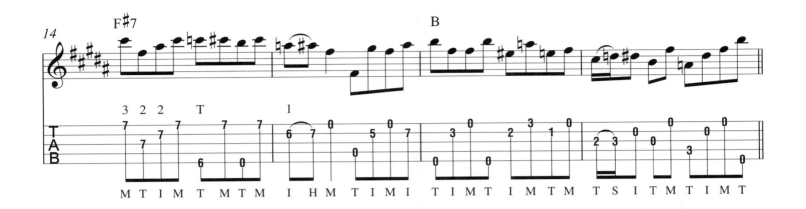

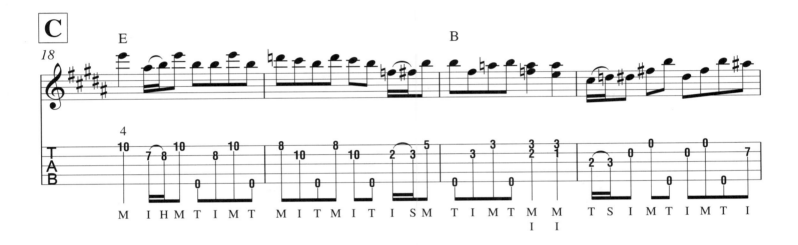

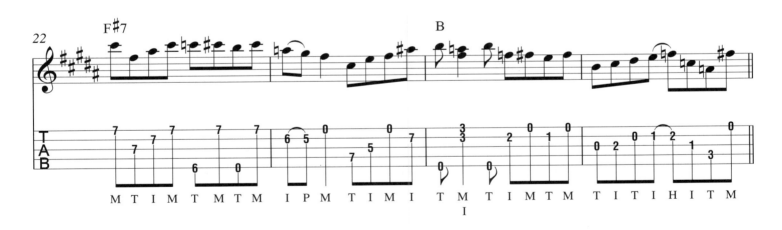

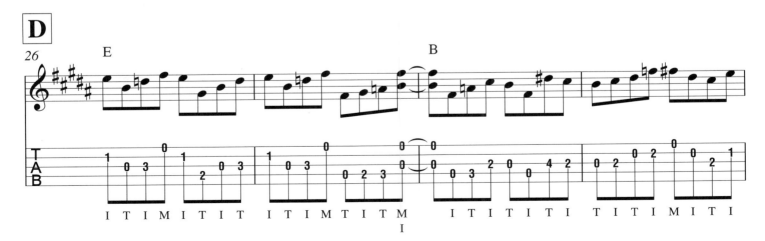

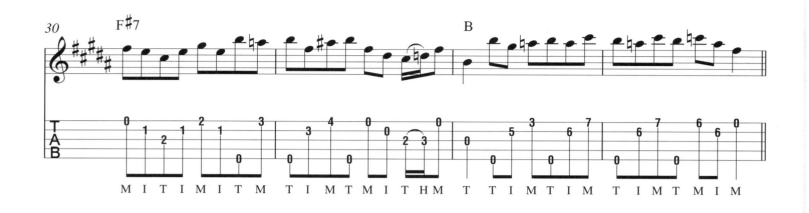

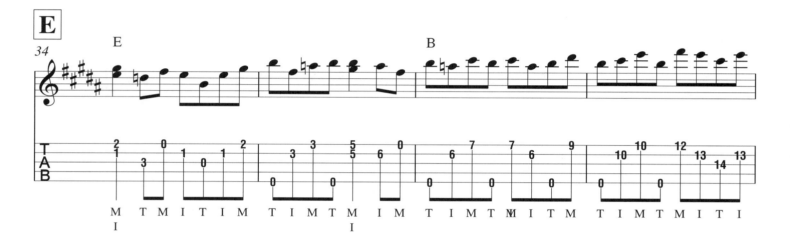

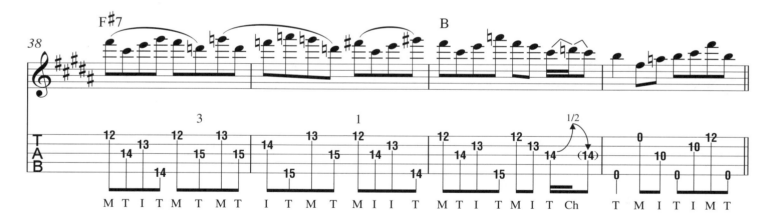

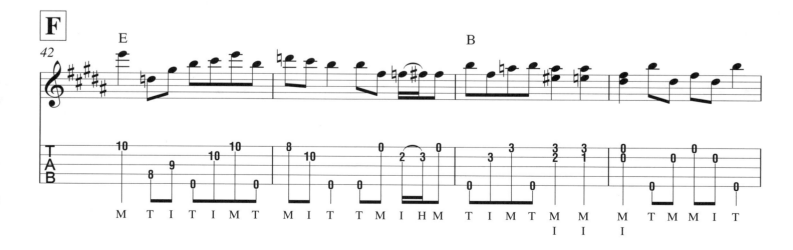

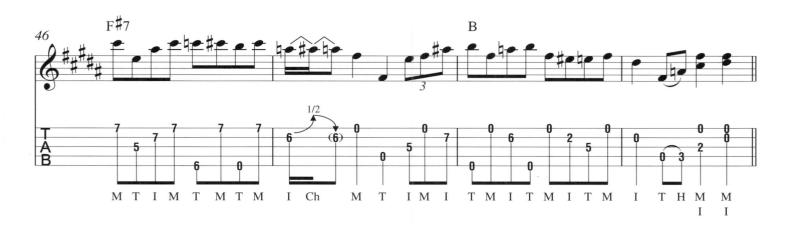

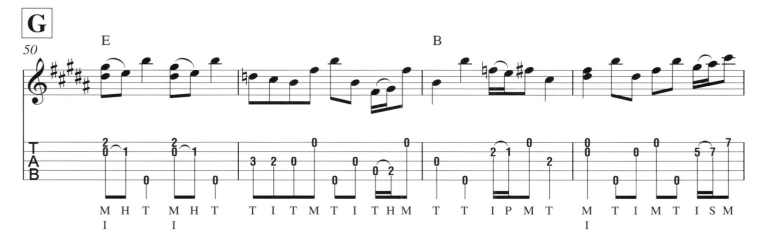

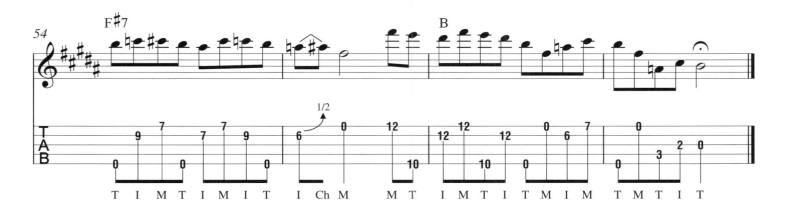

Hot Lick Fiddle Chick (Constantly Flowing Eighth Notes)

I wrote "Hot Lick Fiddle Chick" for a friend of mine, Jen Chapman, who, as an adult, decided to take up the violin and become a professional bluegrass fiddler. I told her that although I thought this was a difficult task, I would do my best to help her realize her dream. She was completely obsessed with bluegrass, and to play bluegrass, you must be comfortable playing in the key of B major. Hence, this tune.
—M.G.

By the way, Jen got quite good and was able to play gigs. "Hot Lick Fiddle Chick" begins clearly in the bluegrass idiom, but by the last eight bars or so, it morphs into a twisted bebop tune. The last section is a really challenging finger-twister on banjo!

The bridge of the tune, which begins in bar 17, introduces more chromaticism, including single and double chromatic-approach tones. This means that you approach a target note from either one or two half steps away. For instance, the phrase in bar 21 is an example of single chromatic approaches into chord tones. The two pickup notes prior to bar 19 are an example of double chromatic-approach tones, as is the phrase in bar 27. The last four bars of the tune are heavily chromatic, using a lot of standard bebop language, including the ♭9 and ♯9 scale degrees.

An interesting aspect of fiddle music is that some notes don't fit neatly into a western scale. Matt notated measures 2, 6, and 10 with a D♯ and F natural, but actually plays notes that "fall in the cracks" between a major 3rd D♯ and minor 3rd D, a little closer to D♯ than to D. And no, he wasn't just playing out of tune! We could call that note a "flat D♯," but fiddle players already have a name for it. It is called a *neutral third*. He does the same thing with the Fs. They are between F and F♯, a little closer to F♯. While this is no problem on fiddle, it creates a bit of a dilemma on banjo and other fretted instruments. Sometimes, you can bend a string, but that isn't always possible. I find the solution is to choose notes that approximate or "imply" the sound. I've also noticed that the *combinations* you use can be the key.

To illustrate this, I played those measures two ways. In the first chorus, I used D♯ and F. The second time through the tune, I reversed that and played D and F♯. I think both ways sound better than altering both notes at the same time. You be the judge.

 "Hot Lick Fiddle Chick" Full Band
TRACK 17

 "Hot Lick Fiddle Chick" Play Along
TRACK 18

Hot Lick Fiddle Chick

gDGBd
Capo 4

Matt Glaser
Arr. Dave Hollender

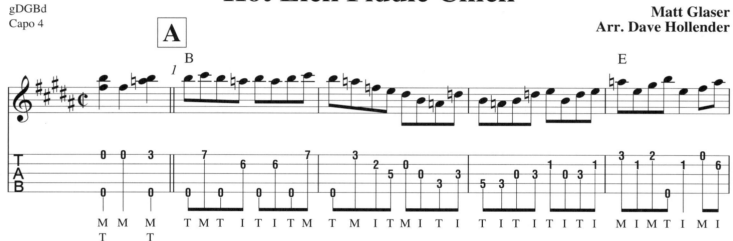

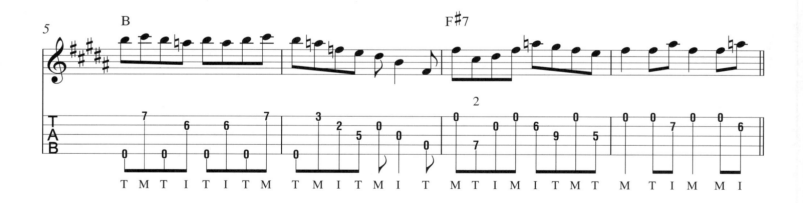

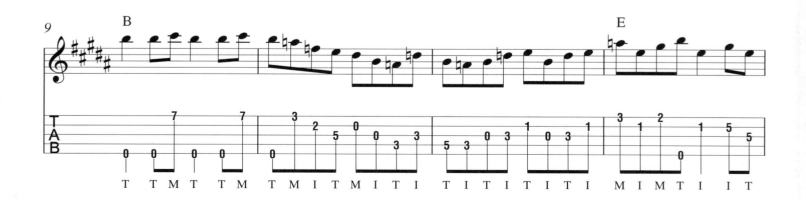

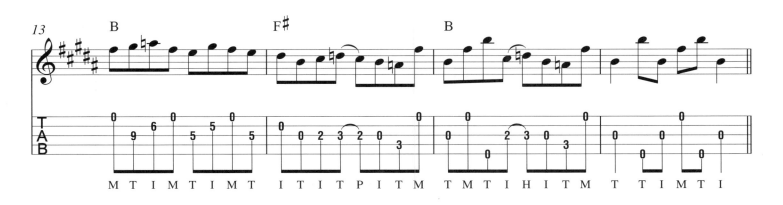

B

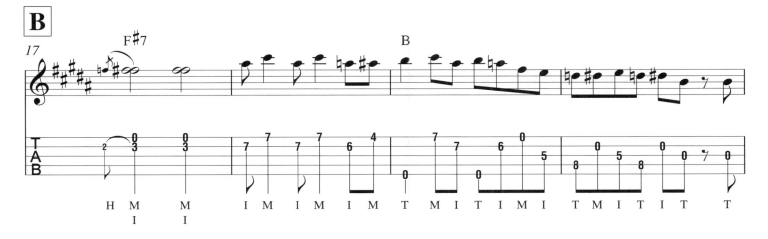

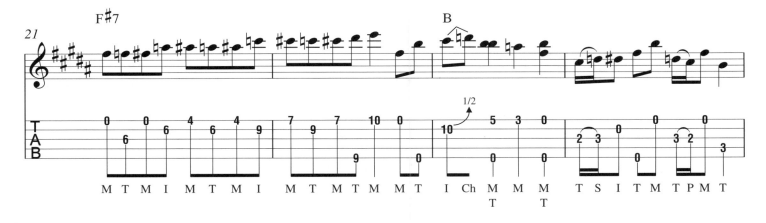

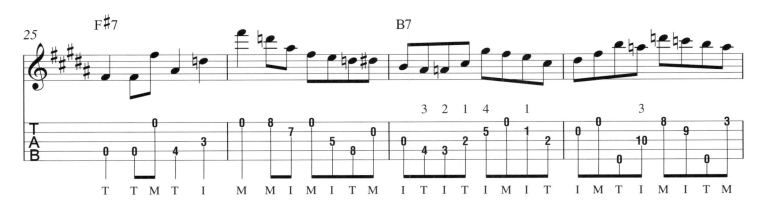

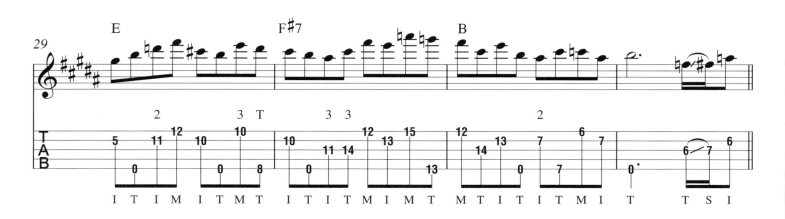

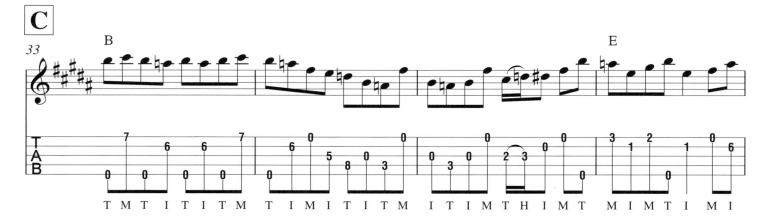

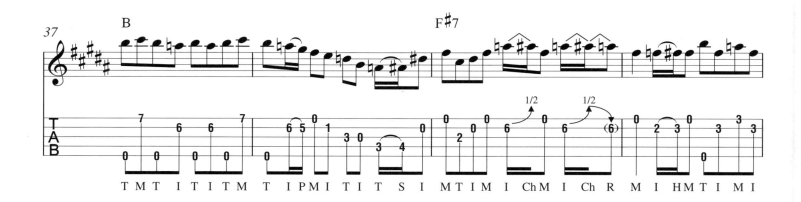

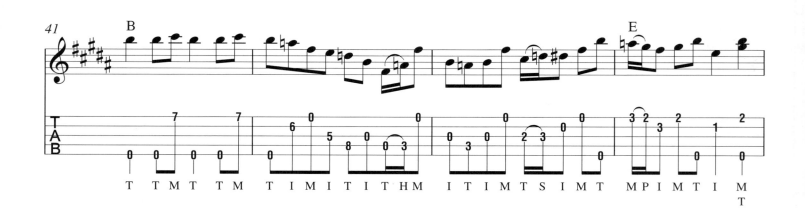

CHAPTER 9

Gunshot Wound in the E.R. (Dominant 7th Chords around the Cycle)

A dear friend of mine, Dr. Kalev Freeman, is a fine fiddler who is an emergency room physician in his day job. Kalev would often come over to my house to play tunes right after he got off his shift in one of Boston's busy emergency rooms. He would always gleefully regale me with horrifying tales of the previous day's festivities in the E.R. One day, he told me a story about a man whose girlfriend was angry with him and shot him in the chest. The man survived, miraculously, and is no worse for wear. I thought that story deserved a tune, and hence we have my "emergency eighth-note etude," "Gunshot Wound in the E.R."

—M.G.

The main concept behind this tune is the rapid arpeggiation of dominant-7th chords in first inversion, going around the cycle of fifths. You should, of course, have committed to memory the notes in the cycle of fifths.

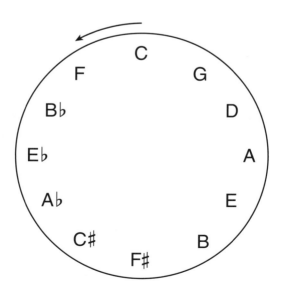

The A section uses all closed fingerings that make it easy to visualize the arpeggios and how the chords intersect when moving through the cycle. There are actually many fingering options, and I encourage you to experiment, but keep these guidelines in mind.

When choosing fingerings, always consider three things.
- Economy of motion
- Fluidity of movements
- Timbre

If it sounds choppy, check for extraneous movements like "flying fingers," lifting and replacing fingers that should stay down, or lifting fingers too early. Plan on starting under tempo and gradually building up speed. If problems recur, repeat the process many times, and it will improve.

"Single-string" technique usually consists of constantly alternating thumb-index; however, I prefer to do it a little differently. I find that using mainly index and middle on the 1st string has some advantages in that you don't have to reposition your hand to reach the string with your thumb[1], as well as reducing the number of times you must cross the thumb and index finger. It also keeps the thumb free for notes on the other strings. Once you get it going, it will become intuitive, and you will rarely ever think about it.

In the second time through, I switched to chords, matching most rhythms with the guitar. The chord voicings are three-note voicings, with the 7th and 3rd on the bottom (played on the 3rd and 4th strings) plus one more chord tone on the 1st string. Take the time to analyze the notes of each chord and how the voice leading works. The way they move eliminates the need to jump up and down the neck when changing chords.

Root movement up a fourth or down a fifth is at the core of harmonic motion in western music. If you can master this most basic of all chord changes, you will have grasped the simple but indispensable message that jazz has bequeathed to bluegrass.

---

1   Although it isn't what we usually think of as "single-string" playing per se, in some old videos you can see that Earl Scruggs used this picking pattern for some of his classic up-the-neck backup licks.

TRACK 19   "Gunshot Wound in the E.R." Full Band

 TRACK 20   "Gunshot Wound in the E.R." Play Along

Gunshot Wound in the E.R.

Matt Glaser
Arr. Dave Hollender

gDGBd

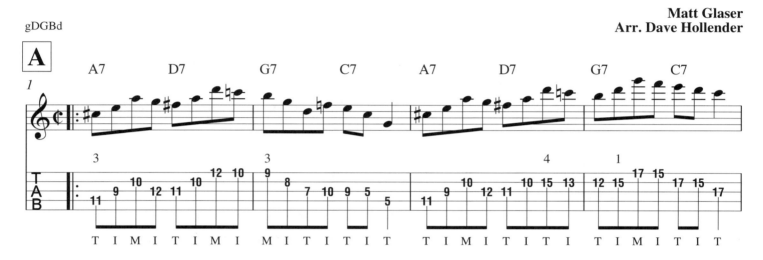

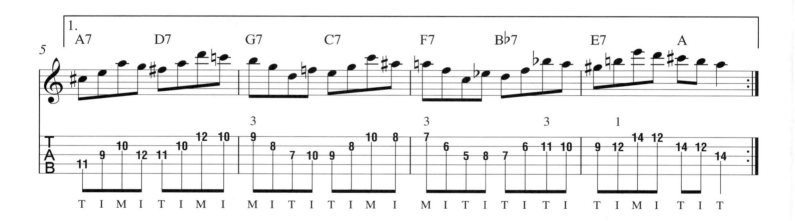

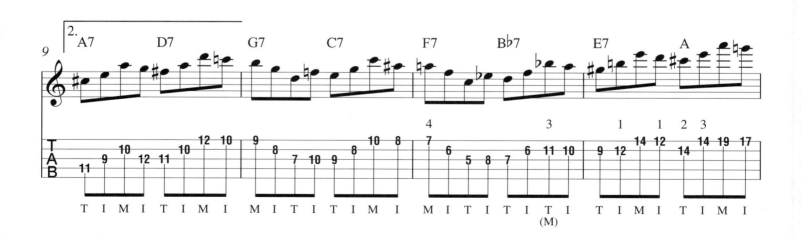

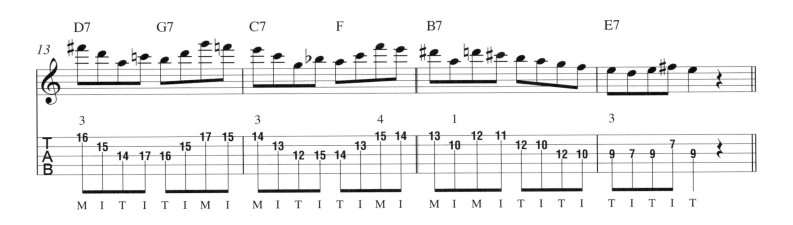

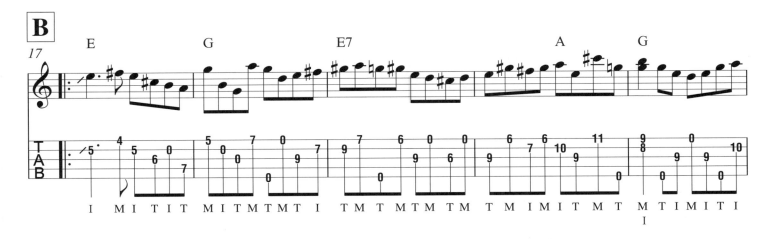

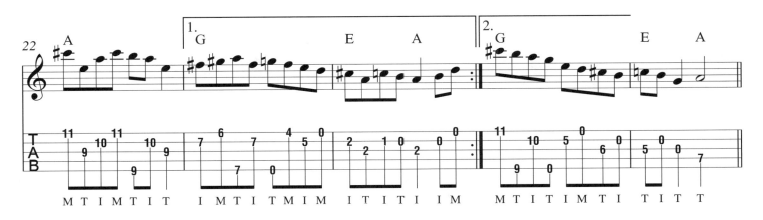

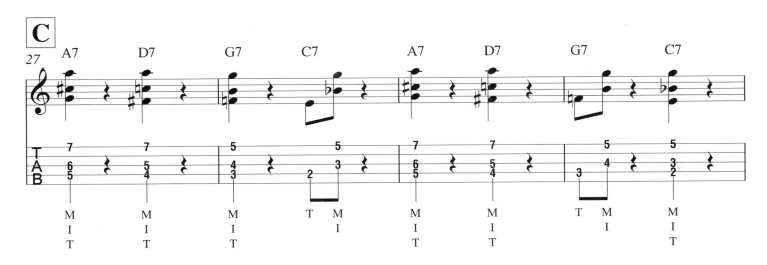

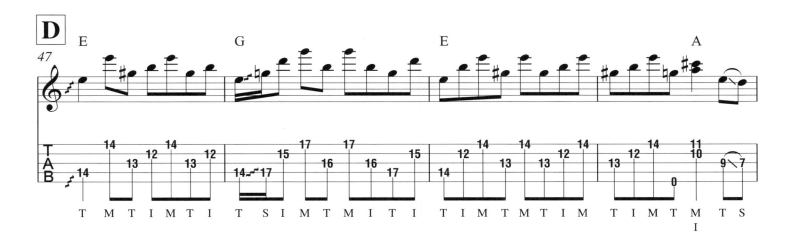

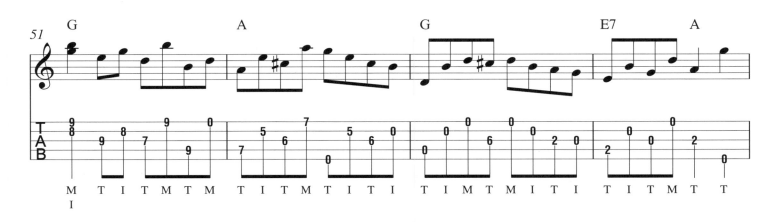

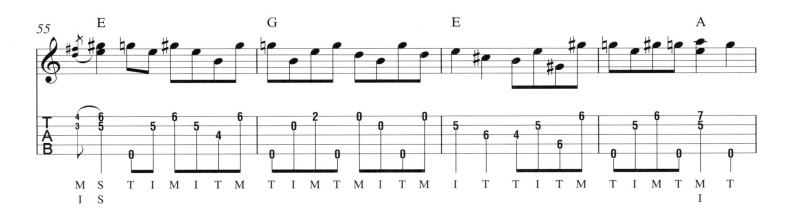

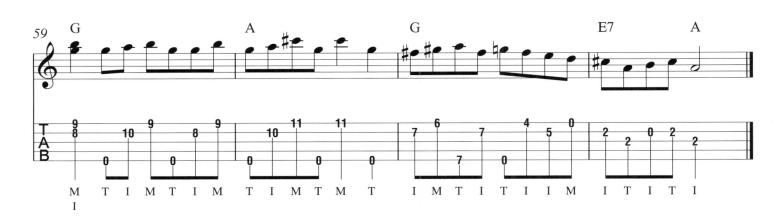

CHAPTER 10

Fishy Hornpipe (Tetrachords)

Continuing with our tradition of smart-alecky harmonic slight of hand to make tunes more interesting, we have "Fishy Hornpipe." The traditional fiddle tune "Fisher's Hornpipe" is usually played in the key of D major, but sometimes it's played in the key of F major. Each key has its own particular sound, as well as its own particular benefits and drawbacks.

> *Because I apparently have too much time on my hands, it occurred to me*
> *that one could play the tune in the keys of D and F simultaneously. Or, if*
> *not simultaneously, then sequentially.*
> —M.G.

So what we have in "Fishy Hornpipe" are four bars in the key of D, then the next four bars in the key of F, and so on and so forth like that.

As if it were not already challenging enough to play fiddle tunes in these keys on banjo, we get to go back and forth every four bars too. Actually, it is a really fun way to play the tune, and the points where the keys intersect are so perfect that we don't understand why the tune wasn't written this way to begin with!

We included some options and variations for playing the tune that involve moving between different octaves.

Matt recommends practicing the lower and upper *tetrachords*—the first or last four notes of the scale, respectively, in both keys. The lower tetrachord of D major is D, E, F♯, and G. The upper tetrachord in D major is A, B, C♯, and D.

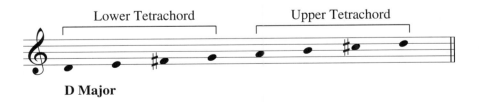

D Major

A *tetrachord* is named as it is because it is a scale comprised of four notes: a whole step from D to E, a whole step from E to F♯, and a half step from F♯ to G.

The tetrachords in F are as follows: lower is F, G, A, and B♭, upper is C, D, E, and F.

Get used to practicing tetrachords. They can really orient your hand to the melodic area in which you'll be improvising.

 "Fishy Hornpipe" Full Band
TRACK 21

 "Fishy Hornpipe" Play Along
TRACK 22

Fishy Hornpipe

Matt Glaser
Arr. Dave Hollender

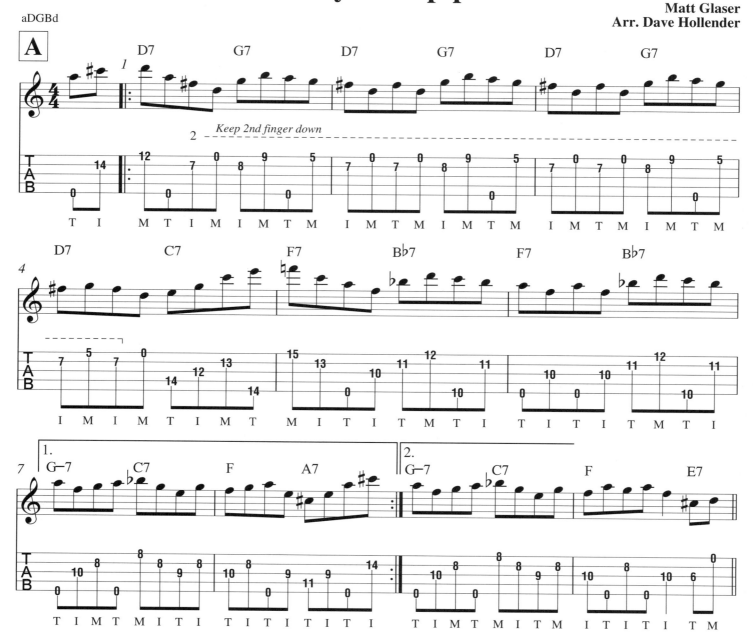

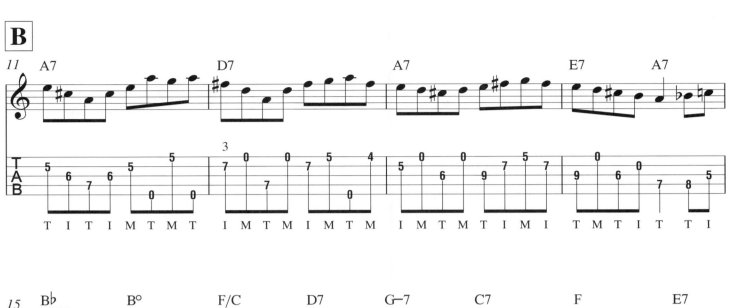

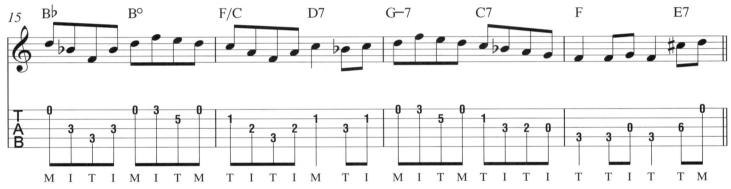

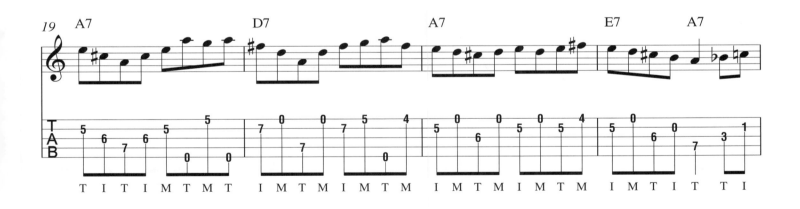

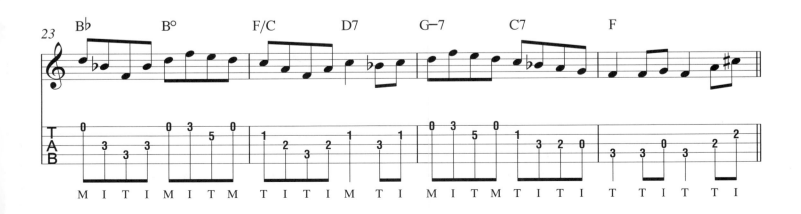

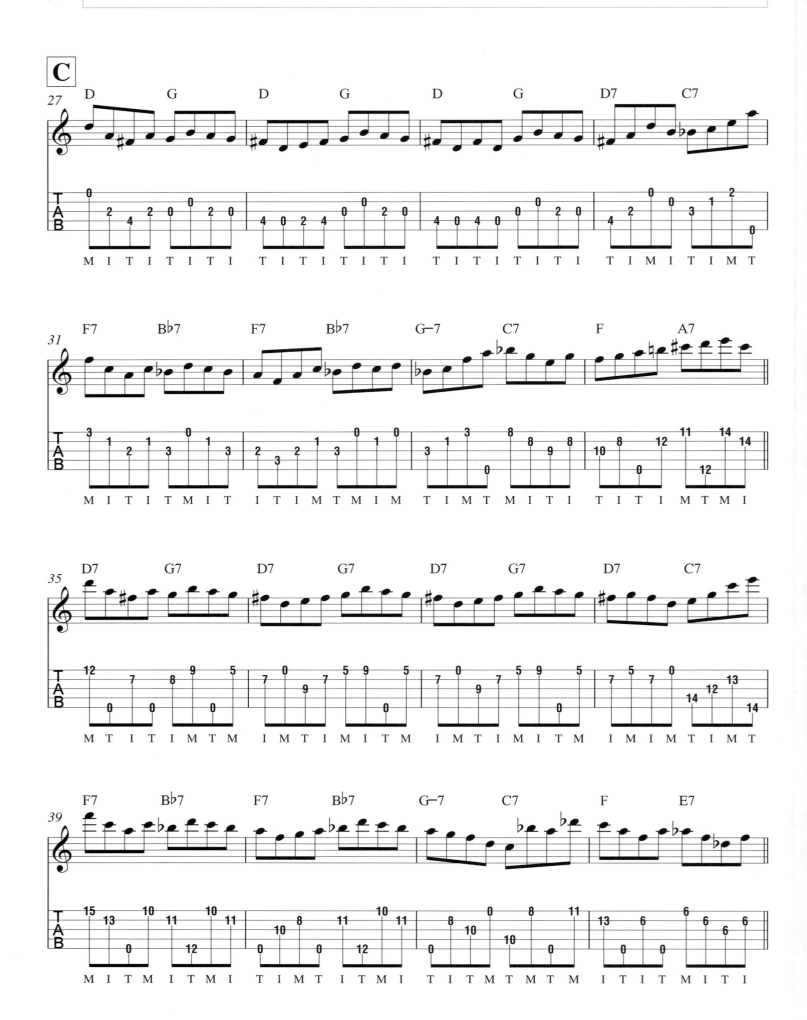

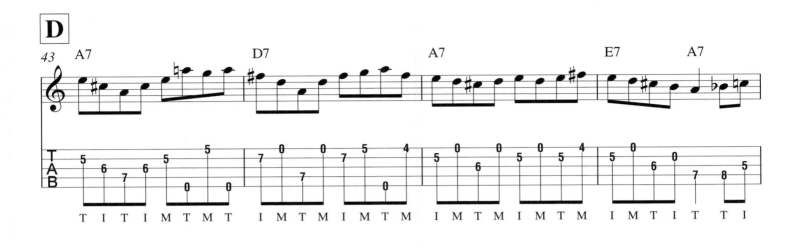

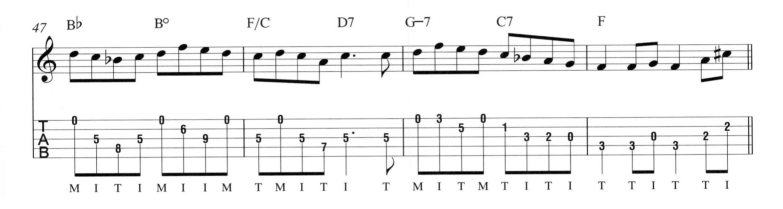

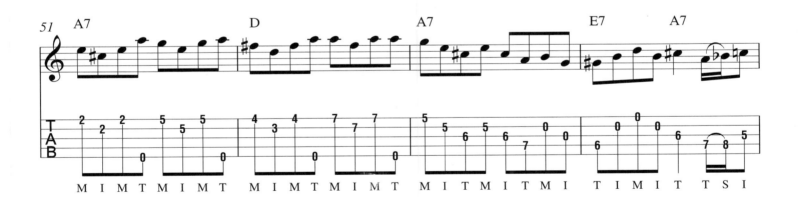

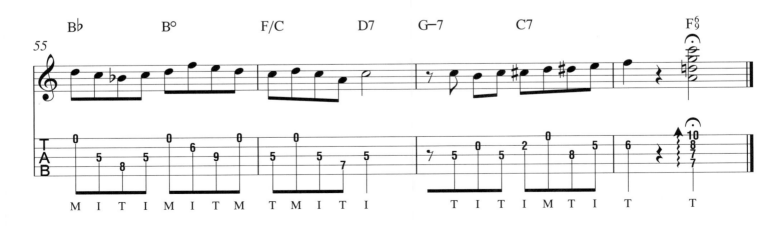

CHAPTER 11

The Girl I Left Behind Me (Solo Banjo with Reharmonization)

In addition to using reharmonization as a technique where chords are added to a tune to generate *motion*, "reharms" can be a great way to reflect or create *emotion*. Unexpected chords can raise listeners' sense of expectations, make the familiar sound less familiar, or even totally transform the meaning of a song.

While traditional music tends to focus more on rhythm and melody than on chords, reharmonizing simple traditional melodies is not unprecedented. When pianist/singer Mose Allison recorded *You Are My Sunshine*, the chords he played seemed to reverse the meaning of the words and transform it into a heartsick love song. The twentieth century English composer Ralph Vaughan Williams wrote a piece called *Six Studies in English Folk-Song* (1926), for cello and piano, in which he set old melodies to rich sounding chords that are guaranteed to evoke ecstasy from listeners.

Since it sometimes isn't possible to play every note of complex chords on banjo, you need to learn which notes need to be there and which ones to omit. For a chord to sound major or minor, you need to include the 3rd. The 7th is important too, especially on dominant 7th chords. Unless you are the bass player, the roots and 5ths are less important, the exception being for playing certain stylistic rhythm patterns like a typical Scruggs-style bass and chord vamp.

It isn't possible to include complete explanations of the basis of every chord choice in this arrangement, but the key thing to notice is that the chords I used always include the melody note of the tune either as a chord tone or a *tension*[1] like the 9th, 11th, or 13th.

Rhythmically, play this version very freely. There is definitely still rhythm, but it is not the kind of metronomic time we are used to playing on banjo. The time should feel *elastic*, leaning forward and then backwards in places, with little pauses at the end of phrases. If you sing the phrases to yourself, you will naturally know where to breathe, and that's the key to making the tune sound expressive.

---

1   Tensions are notes that add color or complexity to chords. They sound "good" because they don't clash with the other notes or unintentionally change that chord's harmonic function.

TRACK 23

"The Girl I Left Behind Me" Solo Banjo

The Girl I Left Behind Me
for Solo Banjo

gDGBd

Dave Hollender

DAVE'S CONCLUSION

The great trumpeter Dizzy Gillespie is often attributed as saying, "You've got to have one foot in the past and one foot in the future." Banjo players have sometimes had a penchant for embracing slavish imitation of Earl Scruggs, but in fairness, we are not alone. A desire to acknowledge revered musical heroes and favorite performances is only natural, and it has led musicians in every musical style to do so the same. Fortunately, there are players who have chosen not to just absorb Earl's contributions to the banjo vernacular (he created 98 percent of it!), but also to take inspiration from his *creative spirit* and willingness to be adventurous. Of Béla Fleck's many accomplishments, one that stands out is that he holds the record for nominations for Grammys in more categories than any musician. Now, newer players are following *that* tradition, and I am confident that Earl approves.

I'd like to thank Matt Glaser for asking me to be a part of this project. It has been a very rewarding process to arrange and play this music. Thanks to Margaret Mackay for her help checking tablature. I hope everyone who studies this book will use what they have learned.

It would be impossible to list every musician and teacher who has influenced me but I'd like to acknowledge and thank Tony Trischka and Bill Keith for contributions each has made to banjo playing and teaching, and for the generosity they have shown. I'd also like to thank Roger Brown, president of Berklee College of Music, whose support was instrumental to the creation of the American Roots Music Program and to opening the doors to banjo and mandolin students at Berklee.

—Dave Hollender

MATT'S CONCLUSION

I hope you have enjoyed playing these etudes, and I hope they help you to have fun solving whatever technical and musical challenges come your way. Having a lifelong creative relationship with your instrument is one of the best ways to ensure a healthy, happy life. I know this because I have been lucky enough to be friends with many of the great fiddlers and jazz violinists who have lived and thrived into their ninth decade. In closing I'd like to dedicate this book to some of these fine gentlemen:

Joe Venuti
Stephane Grappelli
Svend Asmussen
Claude Williams
Johnny Frigo
Johnny Gimble

I am not fit to tie their shoelaces, but I am very thankful that I got to know these men in this lifetime.

Thank you, keep fiddling, and don't hesitate to contact me if you have any questions.

—Matt Glaser

About the Authors

Dave Hollender

Dave Hollender leads a busy musical life in Boston playing and teaching banjo and bass.

As a teen, he moved with his family to Nashville where he began playing the banjo. Some years later, he wanted to study music in a college program and banjo was not an option. So, instead he studied the bass while in school, earning a bachelor's degree from Berklee in 1983, and a master's degree two years later from New England Conservatory. In time, Dave became equally at home playing bluegrass, jazz, and classical music.

Dave is the first banjo teacher at Berklee. He joined the faculty at Berklee College of Music in 1987.

Photo by Charles Cross

Once there, he used his position to advocate for the introduction of banjo as a principal instrument at Berklee and has been instrumental in the growth of acoustic music. He introduced bluegrass to Berklee's ensemble program and wrote the banjo curriculum.

He has played at Carnegie Hall, the Country Music Hall of Fame, Symphony Hall in Boston, and the Montreal and Ottawa Jazz Festivals. He has performed with the Wayfaring Strangers, Darol Anger, Alan Bibey, Emory Lester, Mark Johnson, Haneke Cassel, Casey Driesen, Mike Hartgrove, Charlie Haden, Joe Williams, Chris Connor, Diana Krall, J. Geils, Claude Williams, Ernestine Anderson, Byron Stripling, the Shangri-La's, and Patti Page. As a member of the Boston Philharmonic bass section, Dave played with Yo Yo Ma, Giles Apap, William Warfield, and Sharon Isbin.

Matt Glaser

Photo by Nancy Adler

Matt Glaser is the artistic director of the American Roots music program at Berklee College of Music, and before that, had been chairman of the string department at Berklee for twenty-eight years. Matt is the first and only recipient of the Stephane Grappelli Memorial Award, "In recognition of his significant contribution to the teaching and playing of improvised string music in America," presented by the American String Teachers Association with the National School Orchestra Association. He has performed widely in a variety of idioms ranging from jazz to bluegrass to early music.

Matt has published four books on contemporary violin styles, including *Jazz Violin* co-authored with the late Stephane Grappelli. He has written for many newspapers and music magazines including *Village Voice*, *Strings*, and *Acoustic Musician.* He has performed with Stephane Grappelli, David Grisman, Lee Konitz, Bob Dylan, J. Geils, Leo Kottke, Joe Lovano, Charlie Haden, Michael Brecker, Kenny Werner, Alison Krauss, Bela Fleck, the Waverly Consort, Fiddle Fever, and most recently with Wayfaring Strangers—a band that fuses jazz and folk music. *The Boston Herald* called him "possibly America's most versatile violinist."

Matt served on the board of advisors of the Ken Burns' *Jazz* documentary, and appears in the film as a talking head. He serves on the board of directors of Chamber Music America and the American String Teachers Association.

Matt has performed at the White House and at Carnegie Hall with Yo-Yo Ma and Mark O'Connor as part of Stephane Grappelli's eightieth birthday concert. He has taught at the Mark O'Connor Fiddle Camp, University of Miami, American String Teachers Association conferences, International Association of Jazz Educator conferences, and many others.